GUIDE TO IMPLEMENTING AFRIKAN-CENTERED EDUCATION

by

Kwame Kenyatta

PHOTO CREDITS

pp 8, National Archives; pp 15, Tonya Leigh; pp 19, Courtesy of Amy Job, William Paterson College; pp 21?; pp 23, The AVID Ceneter, pp 28, Tonya Leigh, pp 29, Courtesy of Dr. Molefi Asante, Anthony Browder and Queen Tiye, pp 51 top, Toyna Leigh, pp 51 bottom, National Archives; pp 52, A/P WideWorld Photos; pp 53, *The Ramapo News*; pp 72, Courtesy of Doreen Smith; pp 76, Courtesy of Dr. Clifford Watson; pp 77, Courtesy of Malcolm X Academy; pp 79, Courtsy of G. Holmes Braddock Sr. High School

DEDICATION

This book is dedicated to Afrikan-centered educators, parents, and students everywhere.

ACKNOWLEDGMENTS

I would like to acknowledge Dahia Shabaka, Director of Social Studies, Detroit Public schools, Dr. Kay Lovelace, Associate Superintendent of Philadelphia's Public Schools, Dr. Clifford Watson, Principal of Malcolm X Academy, Detroit Public Schools, Sister JoAnn Watson, President of The Black Media Group, and the Peoples Publishing Group.

SPECIAL THANKS

I would like to thank Sister DeBorah Abdul-Mateen for typing the manuscript; special thanks to Monifa Kenyatta for her loving support.

ISBN   0-9658441-0-2

© 2002 Black Star Press
19410 Livernois Ave
Detroit, MI 48221

Printed in the United States of America.

10   9   8   7   6   5   4

TABLE OF CONTENTS

INTRODUCTION

The information in this guide is designed to assist educators, parents, and students in the implementation of Afrikan-centered education in public schools. It is important to understand from the very beginning that Afrikan-centered education in the public school is different from Afrikan-centered education in independent black institutions. Therefore, the Afrikan-centered curriculum in the public school will not be as strong as the one in the independent school. I consider the public school system the contested zone and the independent school system the liberated zone. In the liberated zone you can do whatever is necessary to educate the students. In the contested zone you are in constant battle with the forces of the status quo. The information in this guide will help you implement and maintain Afrikan-centered education in the public school.

The three articles in the appendix will give you an understanding of how Afrikan-centered education started in Detroit. In Dr. Kay Lovelace's article, "The Last Child," she talks about the black studies program of the 60s and 70s and how ethnic studies was used to dilute the black studies curriculum; much like multiculturalism is used to dilute the Afrikan-centered curriculum. Dr. Lovelace talks about how the African American child has become the last child to be considered in the American education system. Dr. Clifford Watson, principal of *Malcolm X Academy* in Detroit, concentrates on providing background information on the establishment of Afrikan-centered academies in Detroit. The article by Malik Yakini talks about the fundamentals of Afrikan-centered education and how to apply them. The article written by myself highlights some of the national attacks on Afrikan-centered education. I also talk about the importance of Afrikan-centered education for the twenty-first century.

This guide also contains ten keys to developing Afrikan-centered schools. My goal is to help educators and parents who are interested in starting new schools with an Afrikan-centered curriculum. The guide continues, focusing on implementation and Afrikan-centered criteria for school board members, superintendents, teachers, parents, and students. The guide concludes by presenting information on the Detroit model for Afrikan-centered education. The Detroit Public School System is currently the only school system in

INTRODUCTION

the country with a resolution mandating Afrikan-centered education and making it an objective of the school district.

In order for Afrikan-centered education to work in a school district, it must have the full support of the Board of Education. The board should set policy directing the superintendent to develop a comprehensive Afrikan-centered education program that includes research and curriculum development, staff development, curriculum guides, an implementation time line, and other resources needed for curriculum development and implementation. The board must provide real support by way of funding and other material resources. Board members show staff that Afrikan-centered education is a priority by their personal support at the school level.

Once the board has acted by creating an Afrikan-centered policy, the superintendent must then direct his or her staff to develop and implement the policy. The superintendent must let it be known that he or she is committed to the success of Afrikan-centered education. If Afrikan-centered education is an objective and a priority in the school district, it is then tied to the performance of the superintendent and his or her staff.

Parents can make sure that Afrikan-centered education is implemented in the school by checking the books and other material resources that their children use in school and bring home. Parents should visit the school to make sure that the Afrikan-centered education criteria are being implemented. Parents can support the school in an important way by creating an Afrikan-centered home environment.

It is my hope that this guide will provide helpful information and inspiration to all those who are interested in promoting and preserving Afrikan-centered education.

The future of our children will be determined by what we do today. You have taken the first step by buying and reading this guide.

Asante Sana,

Kwame Kenyatta

TOWARD AFRIKAN-CENTERED EDUCATION

Kwame Kenyatta
Board Member at-Large
Detroit Board of Education

The Afrikan-centered thrust in education has sparked national enthusiasm, debate, and attack. People of Afrikan descent see this as a dream come true. However, others see Afrikan-centrism as an attack on American fundamentalism. American fundamentalism can be defined as a Eurocentric world view based on the myth of white supremacy. In other words, the fundamental principles of education in America are rooted in the theory that whites are superior and that all people of color are inferior.

This myth of white supremacy laid the foundation for *manifest destiny* and *eminent domain*, thereby giving justification for the annihilation of the Native American and the enslavement of the Afrikan. I submit to you that the miseducation, marginalization, and outright neglect of children of Afrikan descent and other children of color is done by design and not by accident.

The attacks on Afrikan-centered education since 1994 have been concerted and consistent. We have seen everything from books, national magazines, and newspaper articles charging Afrikan-centrism with the "disuniting" and "fraying" of America. Arthur Schlesinger, the author of *The Disuniting of America,* and Diane Ravitch, author of *The Troubled Crusade,* are the lead gladiators in the fight against Afrikan-centered education. Schlesinger charges that Afrikan-centered education is un-American and promotes the teaching of inaccurate history and distorted facts from a different cultural viewpoint. Diane Ravitch argues that Afrikan-centrism is "particularism that is spreading like wildfire through the education system, promoted by organizations and individuals with a political and professional interest in strengthening ethnic power bases."

These two and other defenders of white supremacy are working overtime to prevent the masses of the people from knowing the truth. They have attempted to discredit Afrikan historians such as Dr. Leonard Jeffries, Dr. Molefi Asante, Dr. Asa Hilliard, Dr. John Henrik-Clark, and others. All of this is designed to convince both blacks and whites that Afrikan-centrism is nothing more than an Afrikanized curriculum. The point that Schlesinger makes about Afrikan-centrism being un-American is true. He states himself that "European ideas and culture founded the Republic . . . and the U.S. is an extension of European civilization." Afrikan-centrism, therefore, provides an opposing worldview to the European ideas and culture that laid the foundation for the oppression of Afrikan people and other people of color. However, being un-American doesn't mean being untrue unless you are operating from a European frame of reference, in which case anything and anyone opposed to the European way of life becomes *untrue.*

In an article that appeared in the *Wall Street Journal* on April 23, 1990, Schlesinger argues that Native Americans and persons of Afrikan descent should be able to assimilate like the Russians, Jews, French, Germans, and Irish immigrants who are now U.S. citizens. But Schlesinger ignores the fact that Russians, Jews, French, Germans, and Irish immigrants were not oppressed and exploited because of their color, nor were they enslaved for more than five-hundred years for the same reason. Native Americans and Afrikans, on the other hand, were and are oppressed and exploited because of their color. It is clear that assimilation of people of color never has been and never will be a reality in America as it stands today.

Afrikan-centrism is much more than mere historical facts and figures centered around time and space. Afrikan-centrism is based on the principle of *Ma'at,* which is truth, justice, balance, and order. Afrikan-centered education brings order by teaching truth in a balanced manner. We are not only talking about content but process as well.

Students are centered around their own cultural life experiences. The classroom is transformed into a holistic learning environment with the student at the center. Afrikan-centered education benefits

▲ Teaching in the round

all students in that it is based on the principles of *Ma'at;* however, the overall thrust of Afrikan-centered education is around the re-centering of children of Afrikan descent.

The education of Afrikan children is fundamental to the continual survival and liberation of Afrikan people. As a people, we have been trained to accept our oppression and the will of the oppressors. As I stated before, educational system in America is designed to promote and advance a racist and capitalistic agenda, an agenda that trains us to become dysfunctional in a society that is hostile to our very existence, an agenda that trains us to be employees and consumers who always work for and buy from someone else, an agenda that allows our children to graduate high school not knowing how to read, write, or do basic math, not to mention how to think.

Many of our children do not graduate; they simply drop out. They become statistics at juvenile centers, group homes, foster care, adoption agencies, prison yards, and graveyards. Our children are referred to by such code names as "at risk" and "inner city youths." They are at risk because they have been targeted for failure.

As we move toward the twenty-first 21st century, we cannot continue to accept this Eurocentric definition of education. Education for our children must be based on the principles of self-determination. We will define, defend, and develop what is in our best interest. Afrikan-centered education is in our best interest. Afrikan-centered education will instill in our youths a sense of self-confidence, pride, and responsibility. It will replace the "dog-eat-dog" and "do-your-own-thing" mentality with a sense of respect for all people.

Afrikan-centered education incorporates the unique learning style of children of Afrikan descent and tends to respect the learning styles of other nationalities. The learning style of the Afrikan child is crucial to the fundamental development of the child. According to the findings of Dr. Asa Hilliard, Professor of Education at Georgia State University, and other Afrikan-centered scholars, there is a difference between the Eurocentric style of teaching and the Afrikan child style of learning.

The Eurocentric style of teaching tends to focus on:

RULES

STANDARDIZATION

CONFORMITY

MEMORY OF SPECIFIC FACTS

REGULARITY

RIGID ORDER

NORMALITY

DIFFERENCES EQUAL DEFECTS

PRECISION

CONTROL

MECHANICAL

"THING" FOCUSED

CONSTANT

SIGN-ORIENTED

DUTY

The Afrikan child's style of learning is centered around:

- FREEDOM
- VARIATION
- CREATIVITY
- MEMORY OF ESSENCE
- NOVELTY
- FLEXIBILITY
- UNIQUENESS
- SAMENESS EQUALS OPPRESSION
- APPROXIMATE
- EXPERIENCE
- HUMANISTIC
- "PEOPLE" FOCUSED
- EVOLVING
- MEANING ORIENTED
- LOYALTY

When the Eurocentric style of teaching comes in conflict with the Afrikan child's style of learning, the Afrikan child is then labeled *nonresponsive* or *hyperactive*. Labeling them *learning disabled (LD)*, and placing Afrikan children in special education and prescribing drugs to speed them up or slow them down is not the answer. The problem is that the Eurocentric style of teaching is in direct contradiction to the Afrikan child's style of learning. The solution to the problem is to end the wholesale use of the Eurocentric teaching style. Eurocentrism is not only alien to the Afrikan child, it is virtually impossible for it to educate him or her because of the historical relationship of oppression and open hostility that continues to exist between Europeans and non-European people. You cannot prepare a child for a liberating life experience using an oppressive philosophy.

Afrikan-centrism will stand and be celebrated as one of the most progressive educational philosophies in the twenty-first century. Afrikan children will no longer see the contributions of their people as a footnote of history, but rather as the center and origin of history.

All children must be centered around their own cultural experiences and allowed to grow to the fullest of their potential.

In conclusion, I would like to say that the implementation of Afrikan-centrism will empower the children of the future with the ability to build a new world that is based on the principles of **MA'AT, TRUTH, JUSTICE, BALANCE,** and **ORDER.**

KEYS TO DEVELOPING SCHOOLS THAT ARE AFRIKAN-CENTERED

The ***Keys to Developing Schools That Are Afrikan-Centered*** are designed to present a step-by-step process to set up or transform schools into Afrikan-centered institutions. If you follow these nine steps closely, you will be well on your way to laying the foundation for an Afrikan-centered school. The two keys that are critical for the success of this process are the leadership team and the curriculum development team. The leadership team provides the fuel to drive this project home. The leadership team should be made up of committed Afrikan-centered educators and parents. The curriculum development team is key because these are the people who plan, train, and implement the curriculum, conduct and modify research to fit the local school plan, and train educators and parents to implement and support the Afrikan-centered curriculum in the school and at home. Parents must be involved in this process if it is to succeed. All of the keys are important, so follow them closely but modify them to fit your school needs.

—Kwame Kenyatta

DEFINE THE MISSION
The mission of the school should articulate the philosophy and the goals. It must be short, yet clear enough so that everyone involved can understand the purpose(s) of the school.

IDENTIFY LEADERSHIP TEAM
This group will act as an advisory council. It will deal with all aspects of the school operations, make recommendations, and conduct a needs assessment related to the overall operation of the program.

PHYSICAL PLANT

The school building and classrooms should reflect and display an Afrikan-centered environment. This should be evident in the hallways, lunchroom, bulletin boards, etc. The seating arrangement should change to reflect a nontraditional room setup with desks in circles or small group settings of 3-5 students.

ESTABLISH AN AFRIKAN-CENTERED CURRICULUM DEVELOPMENT TEAM

This group will conduct research into existing programs, modify research to fit the local school plan, implement seminars and workshops, and develop lessons and curriculum guides for all content areas.

IDENTIFY SITES: EASY ACCESS IS CRITICAL FOR SUCCESS

Schools should be strategically located throughout the district. If this is impossible, then the site should be centrally located. There should be an elementary, middle, and high school site.

IMPLEMENTATION PROGRAM

This program is established by the Afrikan-centered curriculum development team. Each local site will establish an implementation time line.

EVALUATION

Evaluations are essential for an effective program. The community, students, and staff, both instructional and noninstructional, should evaluate the program and make recommendations based on the findings of the evaluation.

REFINE/REIMPLEMENT

The evaluation will help to identify areas to keep, change, or eliminate as the program is refined and reimplemented.

REEVALUATE

Evaluation is a continuous process and must be ongoing for a successful classroom or school program.

CRITERIA FOR AFRIKAN-CENTERED TEACHERS

The ***Criteria for Afrikan-Centered Teachers, Classrooms, Students, and Parents*** is designed to provide minimum standards. Whenever you walk into an Afrikan-centered classroom, you should see the basic items listed in my ***Criteria for Afrikan-Centered Classrooms***, but these are only a foundation on which to build. Afrikan-centered teachers should add to these eight criteria. Students who are taught from an Afrikan-centered perspective are expected to display positive behavior and a high level of discipline and respect. These criteria will help them achieve that expectation.

Just as Afrikan-centered students are expected to display disciplined, respectful behavior, so are Afrikan-centered parents. Afrikan-centered parents should support the school and the students by creating and maintaining an Afrikan-centered home environment, building on the criteria that follow.

—***Kwame Kenyatta***

1. Show Love, Care, and Concern

Afrikan-centered teachers must provide a loving environment in which their students can learn. The teacher must show love, care, and concern for each and every student.

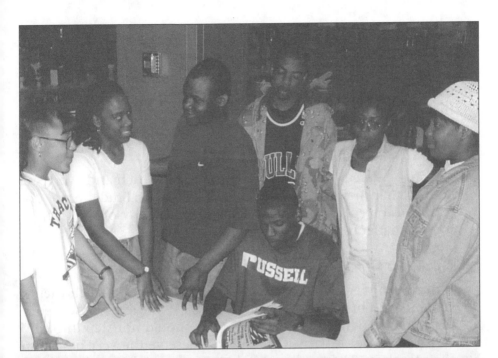

▲ Students learn to share opinions and learn to respect each other in an Afrikan-centered environment.

2. RESPECT ALL STUDENTS

Afrikan-centered teachers respect their students at all times. The teacher respects the students by listening to their concerns and valuing their opinions. All students must be made to feel that they are an important part of the classroom.

3. CALLING STUDENTS BY THEIR NAME

Afrikan-centered teachers work hard to know each and every student so that they can best educate that student. Students are not treated as objects or products. They are the center of the classroom experience.

4. COME TO CLASS PREPARED TO TEACH

Afrikan-centered teachers come to class prepared to teach their students and bring the best out in them. If a teacher is not feeling well or having a bad day, he or she should not step into the classroom or leave early. Our children deserve the very best from their teachers. The teacher should be prepared, know the subject matter, and teach it with love and confidence.

5. MAKE SURE ALL STUDENTS HAVE WHAT THEY NEED TO DO THEIR LESSON

An Afrikan-centered teacher is concerned about the whole child. The teacher will make sure that all students have what they need to do their work, that is, books, paper, pencils, proper dress, and food for the day. If the student is in need of anything, the teacher will make the necessary arrangements and/or contact the appropriate parties to take care of these needs.

6. MAINTAIN CONTACT WITH THE PARENTS OF ALL STUDENTS

Afrikan-centered teachers understand the importance of family and work to maintain regular and frequent contact with all parents. Parents should not only be contacted when their child is doing poorly in class, but they should also be contacted when their child is doing well. The regular progress report and contact with the teacher lets parents know whether their home efforts are helping the child.

7. MAKE SURE THE CLASSROOM IS CLEAN, SAFE, AND SECURE.

An Afrikan-centered teacher practices the principles of *Ujima* (collective work and responsibility). He or she will work with the maintenance crew and security team of the school to keep the classroom clean, safe, and secure.

8. ANSWER ALL QUESTIONS AND EXPLAIN ALL LESSONS COMPLETELY AND CLEARLY.

An Afrikan-centered teacher knows that if students do not understand the questions, they cannot reach the right answers. Many students are afraid to ask questions in class. It is important for the teacher to create an open yet disciplined classroom environment where students can feel free to ask questions and challenge information that is put before them.

CRITERIA FOR AFRIKAN-CENTERED CLASSROOMS

1. ARRANGE CHAIRS IN A CIRCULAR FASHION STARTING FROM EACH END OF THE TEACHER'S DESK

The circle promotes unity and openness in the classroom. Afrikan-centered students are taught to work together and to support each other.

2. DISPLAY AFRIKAN-CENTERED PICTURES AND ARTIFACTS

It is important that students see positive Afrikan images in their learning environment. In order for students to appreciate Afrikan art, they must be exposed to it.

3. DISPLAY THE RED, BLACK, AND GREEN UNIVERSAL AFRIKAN FLAG

The flag promotes nationalism and self-determination by giving the student a sense of identity, purpose, and direction.

4. DECORATE WALLS WITH THE RIGHT COLORS

The color of a room can create either negative or positive moods. Harmonious vibration created by the right color combination such as a spiritual blue, a royal purple, and a loving red can aid in the learning process.

▲ Displaying Afrikan-centered artifacts and materials

5. MAINTAIN A STUDENT ACTIVITIES BOARD

The purpose of the student activities board is to keep students informed on upcoming classroom and school activities (e.g., programs, field trips, and visits to the school by prominent individuals).

6. ESTABLISH AND MAINTAIN A FAMILY WALL OF PRIDE.

When students can look on the wall and see themselves and their family members, they will see the classroom as a part of their family and take ownership of the educational process.

7. MAINTAIN AN AFRIKAN-CENTERED CURRENT EVENTS BOARD

The purpose of this board is to keep students informed about current Afrikan-centered activities taking place in the community and around the country.

8. DISPLAY THE SCHOOL PLEDGE, SONG, MISSION, GOALS, AND OBJECTIVES

This will help students know and understand the pledge, mission, goals and objectives of their school and take pride in the fulfillment of these.

9. MAINTAIN LIVE PLANTS AND CLASSROOM PETS

This will help to provide students with a sense of respect and responsibility for other life forms.

10. MAINTAIN AN AFRIKAN-CENTERED SUGGESTION BOX

Students should be encouraged to make Afrikan-centered suggestions that would improve the quality of the learning in their classroom.

▲ Afrikan-centered learning is a happy experience.

CRITERIA FOR AFRIKAN-CENTERED STUDENTS

1. COME TO CLASS PREPARED TO LEARN

Afrikan-centered students come to school prepared to learn; that is, they have their books, paper, pencils, computer, calculator, etc. ready. Afrikan-centered students understand that they are in school for one purpose only, and that is to learn.

2. RESPECT THE TEACHER AT ALL TIMES

Afrikan-centered students respect their teachers at all times. There is no talking back, name calling, swearing, or any other disruptive behavior allowed.

3. COMPLETE YOUR LESSON IN A TIMELY MANNER.

Afrikan-centered students take pride in completing their lessons neatly and in a timely fashion.

4. RESPECT AND WORK COOPERATIVELY WITH YOUR FELLOW STUDENTS

Afrikan-centered students respect their classmates and work cooperatively with them to achieve academic success. Afrikan-centered students do not engage in name calling, fighting, stealing, or other negative behavior. Afrikan-centered students work with and support each other in the classroom and in the community.

▲ Studying in the spirit of *Ujima* (collective work and responsibility)

5. KEEP YOUR CLASSROOM CLEAN, SAFE, AND SECURE

Afrikan-centered students work with their teacher to keep their classroom clean, safe, and secure. The classroom does not belong to the maintenance people or the security crew. The classroom belongs to the students and their teachers.

6. ASK QUESTIONS, LISTEN CAREFULLY, AND TAKE GOOD NOTES

Afrikan-centered students understand that they are in school for one reason only, and that is to learn. Students listen carefully to the teacher and ask questions when they don't understand. Students take good notes for review during study time.

▲ Taking pride in studying hard and learning much.

7. BE A LIVING EXAMPLE OF THE AFRIKAN-CENTERED (NGUZO SABA) VALUE SYSTEM

Afrikan-centered students who are taught the *Nguzo Saba* will work daily to put them to use. Negative behavior is unacceptable from an Afrikan-centered student. (See page 25.)

8. MAINTAIN A SENSE OF IDENTITY, PURPOSE, AND DIRECTION

Afrikan-centered students know who they are, what their purpose is in life, and in which direction to go to achieve that purpose. Afrikan-centered students are on time, on task, and always on their mission.

9. MAINTAIN INVOLVEMENT IN THE COMMUNITY

Afrikan-centered students are taught and understand the importance of community service. Students volunteer their time and skills to help improve the community in which they live.

THE SEVEN PRINCIPLES OF THE NGUZO SABA

1. **UMOJA** *(Unity)*—To strive for principled and harmonious togetherness in the family, community, nation, and World Afrikan community.

2. **KUJICHAGULIA** *(Self-Determination)*—Defining ourselves, naming ourselves, creating for ourselves, and speaking for ourselves instead of being defined, named, created for, and spoken for by others.

3. **UJIMA** *(Collective Work and Responsibilities)*—Building and maintaining our community together and making our brother's and sister's problems ours to work out together.

4. **UJAMAA** *(Cooperative Economics)*—To build our own businesses, control the economics of the community, and share in all its work and wealth.

5. **NIA** *(Purpose)*—Making our collective goal building up and developing the community, and restoring people to their traditional greatness.

6. **KUUMBA** *(Creativity)*—Leaving the community more vibrant, more vital, and more beautiful than we inherited it.

7. **IMANI** *(Faith)*—Believing in the Creator, our people, our leaders, our teachers, our parents, ourselves, and the righteousness and victory of our struggle.

CRITERIA FOR AFRIKAN-CENTERED PARENTS

1. PROVIDE LOVE, HEALTH, AND SECURITY

An Afrikan-centered parent provides much love and a healthy and secure environment for his or her children.

2. PROVIDE HEALTHY MEALS ON A DAILY BASIS

Afrikan-centered parents make sure that their children receive healthy meals on a daily basis.

3. MAINTAIN A DRUG-FREE ENVIRONMENT

Afrikan-centered homes are free of any and all illegal drugs. The use of any legal drugs is minimized and kept out of reach and sight of children. Children follow the example of their parents; therefore it is important to set a positive example.

4. ESTABLISH AND MAINTAIN A DAILY FAMILY HOUR

Family relationships are the heart of any Afrikan-centered home. A daily family hour that includes all family members is essential. Family members can engage in conversation, games, meditation, dinner, study, exercise, and other activities. Children learn the importance and joy of maintaining family relationships by being included in the daily process.

5. ESTABLISH AND MAINTAIN AFRIKAN-CENTERED FAMILY CEREMONIES

Birthdays, anniversaries, graduations, naming ceremonies, rites of passage, and other ceremonies and holidays reinforce the Afrikan-centered family. In order for Afrikan-centered education to be successful in school, it must be supported by a strong Afrikan-centered home program. Parents are encouraged to celebrate birthdays, anniversaries, graduations and other special family events from an Afrikan-centered perspective.

6. MAINTAIN AN AFRIKAN-CENTERED FAMILY LIBRARY

All Afrikan-centered homes must have a library. We can't tell our children to read when we don't have anything at home for them to read. As parents, we should read and keep ourselves informed on a daily basis. When our children see us reading on a regular basis, they learn that reading is a priority in the home. The children should be introduced to new Afrikan-centered material regularly.

7. VISIT OR CALL YOUR CHILD'S SCHOOL AT LEAST ONCE A WEEK

Afrikan-centered parents take ownership of their children's education. They visit the school on a regular basis and participate in school and community activities. Children of involved parents always do better in school.

8. PROVIDE A COMFORTABLE ENVIRONMENT FOR HOME STUDY

An area should be made available in the home where children can study without being interrupted. Study time is very important and is the key to academic success. Students are encouraged to study at least two hours a night.

9. DISPLAY AFRIKAN-CENTERED PICTURES AND ARTIFACTS IN THE HOME

Our children will develop a greater appreciation for Afrikan-centered art and music if it is provided and displayed on a regular basis in the home.

▲ It takes an entire community to raise a child.

10. MAINTAIN AN AFRIKAN-CENTERED SPIRITUAL ENVIRONMENT

Afrikan-centered parents must encourage their children to establish and maintain a relationship with God and their ancestors. Libations should be poured at all family celebrations. *Imani* (faith) teaches us that spirituality is the foundation of our families and all that we do. We must have faith in God, our ancestors, ourselves, our family, our community, and our people.

GUIDING PRINCIPLES FOR AN AFRIKAN-CENTERED EDUCATION: THE DETROIT MODEL

In this section, the reader will find information on what I call the Detroit model for Afrikan-centered education in the public schools. First is the Afrikan-Centered Resolution which I presented to the Detroit School Board in 1993. The resolution provided the conceptual and instructional foundation for infusing Afrikan-centered education throughout the district. Next are **INDABA** principles, which were developed after intense discussion led by such scholars as Dr. Molefi Asante, Anthony Browder, and Dr. Leonard Jeffries, to name only a few. The discussion group was charged with creating a common knowledge base while developing guiding principles that concentrated on "viewing, reviewing, and cleansing" written information in textbooks and curriculum guides.

The **INDABA** group met during the months of February through July of 1993 and 1994. Since that time, new information has come to light and there is a need to update the **INDABA**, but the majority of the information remains relevant and is provided here for your edification.

—Kwame Kenyatta

Dr. Molefi Asante

Anthony Browder

Dr. Leonard Jeffries

AFRIKAN-CENTERED RESOLUTION: DETROIT PUBLIC SCHOOLS

The Detroit Public School district prepares students for self-determination as contributing and participating members in a culturally diverse world. Students must understand and develop a sense of responsibility to the community so that they will understand and appreciate the totality of society. Positive self-esteem and the valuing of cultural diversity is grounded in historical consciousness which is based on *truth, balance, order, harmony,* and *reciprocity*. Students, parents, and administrators, along with instructional as well as noninstructional staff must be empowered with the vision, tools, skills, and opportunities to create an environment which will not marginalize but instead ensure equity and equality for everyone.

RESOLUTION

WHEREAS the students of the Detroit Public Schools are entitled to an education and curriculum based on *truth, balance, order, harmony,* and *reciprocity* that so each student will understand that self-determination is fundamental for participation in a culturally diverse society;

and

WHEREAS the students must be centered in their own historical and cultural heritage which fosters a positive self-esteem, develops group identity, and provides for entrepreneurial activities that encourage collective work and responsibility;

and

WHEREAS the Detroit Public Schools must therefore assure that the entire curriculum enables Detroit Public School students to develop a knowledge and understanding leading to an appreciation of their own heritage/culture and a respect for cultural diversity;

and

WHEREAS as the Detroit Public Schools must provide the means to coordinate the development and implementation of the curriculum as well as provide for the continuing research of content to ensure *truth, balance, order, harmony,* and *reciprocity* for students, parents, staff, and the community at large;

NOW THEREFORE BE IT RESOLVED that the General Superintendent of the Detroit Public Schools directs staff to (1) develop procedures and guidelines for textbook selection; (2) review all textbooks and instructional materials to ensure that they are accurate, complete, and free of stereotypical views of any group whether expressed or implied by statement, visual image, or omission; and when necessary (3) develop supplementary material when textbooks and other commercially available materials fail to meet guidelines for comprehensive and accurate instruction.

And, be it finally

RESOLVED that the General Superintendent directs the staff of the Detroit Public Schools to develop a comprehensive Afrikan-Centered Education Program which includes research and curriculum development, staff development, Pre-K-12 curriculum guides, an implementation time line, and other resources needed for curriculum development and implementation.

—Adopted February 2, 1993

Detroit Public Schools

INDABA PRINCIPLE ONE: TIME AND PLACE

All humanity developed within the context of *time* and *place*. A knowledge and understanding of time and place will provide a framework for an accurate, comprehensive study of humankind to reflect the universal development of cultures. It is wellresearched and documented that humankind began on the continent of Afrika. As *time* and *place* are studied in an historical context, it can be made clear that the borrowing and mingling of cultures and ideas across boundaries have impacted the development of nations, cultures, and civilizations throughout history.

The concept of *time*, through the use of a time line, illustrates the origin of humankind and pictorially displays the development of civilization, past and present. The use of time lines dramatically reveals at a glance that the domination of Europe (circa C.E./A.D.1400) has only taken place within a brief period of time when compared to the origin of the Nubian (Ta-Seti) civilization circa 4000 B.C.E./B.C.

The concept of *place* refers to location and must be viewed in an historical as well as a contemporary perspective. Afrika is a continent. Egypt is and has historically been a country in Afrika. *Place* helps us understand the differences between physical and political geography; for example, the area designated as North Afrika is a political designation and not a geographic one. By creating a north-south division of Afrika, students are confused about the cultural relatedness of Afrika.

B.C.E.=BEFORE THE COMMON ERA

3.6 million	2.5 million	1 million	200,000	5 500	5 000	4 500	4 100	4 000	3 500	3 100	3 000	2 500	2 000
Older Fossil found in Africa (Lucy)	Homo habilis	Homo erectus (Diaspora begins)	Homo sapiens				TA SETI (oldest known civilization)			KMT Unification			

INDABA PRINCIPLE TWO: DIASPORA

The *Diaspora* is viewed as the population of the earth by indigenous Afrikans through a planned or circumstantial movement from the Afrikan continent approximately 250,000 years ago. Any discussion of the *Diaspora* must begin with the following understanding of archeological and anthropological research.

+ The oldest fossil remains of humankind were discovered in Tanzania on the east coast of Afrika

+ Scientific studies validate the Afrikan continent as the birthplace of humankind and the origin of all human migrations and immigrations.

Current scientific data have affirmed that the dispersion of humankind began in Afrika and that the peoples of the world are descendants of Afrikans. Focusing on the Afrikan *Diaspora,* and the various roles of Africans and African civilizations must be integral parts of any discussion of the arts, sciences, history, mathematics, religion, law, government, agriculture, and all subsequent cultures and civilizations.

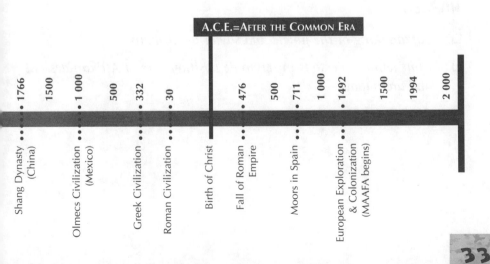

A.C.E.=AFTER THE COMMON ERA

| 1766 | 1500 | 1 000 | 500 | 332 | 30 | | 476 | 500 | 711 | 1 000 | 1492 | 1500 | 1994 | 2 000 |

Shang Dynasty (China) • Olmecs Civilization (Mexico) • Greek Civilization • Roman Civilization • Birth of Christ • Fall of Roman Empire • Moors in Spain • European Exploration & Colonization (MAAFA begins)

INDABA PRINCIPLE THREE: CLEANSING

Cleansing is the elimination of myths, stereotypes, images, pejoratives, and negative expressions that suggest that Afrikan and Afrikan Americans have contributed less to human culture than other people.

MYTHS

❏ *Missionaries brought civilization to Afrika.*

❏ *Cannibalism started in Afrika.*

❏ *Ancient Afrikans had no written languages.*

STEREOTYPES

❏ *Afrikans lack the Puritan work ethic; i.e., they are lazy.*

❏ *Afrikans dance and sing; Europeans build and create.*

❏ *Graduation of skin color has a direct relationship to academic and social status.*

❏ *Afrikans had no written languages.*

IMAGES

❏ *Tarzan, king of the jungle and savior of Afrikans*

❏ *Aunt Jemina: Persons in servitude positions are of Afrikan descent and are happy.*

❏ *Afrikan rain forests are called jungles.*

PEJORATIVES

❏ *"Boy" or "girl" for adults*

❏ *"Nigga/Nigger," "Spook," "Junglebunny," "Coon," "Kaffir," etc.*

❏ *"Pigmy," "Bushman," "Hottentot," "Savage"*

NEGATIVE EXPRESSIONS

❏ *Black* as a negative reference, e.g., black Monday, black death (i.e., a European plague), black magic, blackballed, blacklist

❏ Nappy hair, good hair, bad hair

Because most curricula have been written from a European perspective, the idea that other people existed as subjects rather than objects is seldom discussed or legitimized in any reference. Non-European children grow up internalizing the negative concepts that others have imposed on them. This principle seeks to identify and correct this problem. The process of *cleansing* will stop the dehumanization of people.

INDABA PRINCIPLE FOUR:
MAAFA

Maafa is an Afrikan term meaning the worldwide devastation and scattering of indigenous Afrikan people through captivity and enslavement worldwide. The *Maafa* is the story of:

- ☞ unprecedented human misery and cruelty for four hundred years in the interest of profits and resources which laid the economic foundations of America and Western Europe.

- ☞ international alliances of the religious and political institutions to maximize their resources in the conquest and control of the Afrikan's mind (Afrikan identity), body (slavery), and land.

- ☞ Afrikan resistance as demonstrated by the examples of King Kuselia, Queen Dahia Al-Kahina, Queen Nzinga, King Chaka, the Maroons, and various slave revolts in the Americas.

- ☞ the brutal raiding of Afrikan villages and the kidnapping of Afrikans, the genocide of their culture, and the pillage and co-option of their history by foreigners.

It has been estimated that approximately 100,000,000 Afrikans were imported into the English colonies of America and the West Indies. The mortality rates indicate that one out of three Afrikans died in raids and on the journey to the West Afrikan Atlantic coast. Slave merchants lost one-third of their "human cargo" during the Middle Passage (the voyage across the Atlantic Ocean).

The slave trade was responsible for the deaths of about 40,000,000 Afrikans. The horrible and notorious Middle Passage alone claimed the lives of 15,000,000 to 20,000,000 Afrikans who died in the bowels of slave ships infested with diseases and death.

The *Maafa* must be told so children of all cultures will understand the holocaust of Afrikan people, but most important, children of Afrikan descent will understand that the *Maafa* (holocaust) was a devastating interruption in their history and not the beginning, as is indicated in most textbooks.

INDABA PRINCIPLE FIVE: COMMISSION/OMISSION

Commission/Omission refers to the deliberate distortions and historical misperceptions passed on as historical facts. It is the conscious effort to perpetuate erroneous, undocumented ideas and concepts concerning Africans and other diverse groups. *Commission* does not require the documentation of information. Examples of commission would include, but are not limited to, the following.

COMMISSION

Acts of Commission:

1. **Slaves came from Afrika.**

   THE TRUTH: *Africans came from Afrika and were made into slaves.*

2. **Islam civilized West Afrika.**

   THE TRUTH: *West Afrika was highly civilized prior to the introduction of the Islamic culture. The Islamic culture was introduced in 640 C.E.*

3. **Afrikans did not have a civilization; therefore Afrikans (African Americans) have not made any contributions to the world.**

   THE TRUTH: *The Olduvai Gorge in East Afrika and the Nile Valley have revealed the ruins of major civilizations that were highly sophisticated in their social interactions. They produced monuments that cannot be duplicated even with today's technology.*

4. **Afrikans are as responsible for slavery as any other group and did not resist the oppression of the slave trade.**

   THE TRUTH: *Although there were some Afrikans involved in the slave trade, many Afrikans fought extensive wars to resist foreign invasion and the trade of Afrikans.*

5. **The labeling of Afrika as *the dark continent***

   THE TRUTH: *Afrika gave light to the world through contributions in the areas of science, medicine, art, religion, literature, music, and mathematics.*

OMISSION

Omission is the act of deliberately leaving out information pertaining to non-European groups. The act of omission deprives us of critical data and impairs our ability to analyze world events based on sufficient information. Failure to include the Moorish contributions to the European Renaissance after the fall of the Roman Empire in A.D.476 is an example of omission. Most materials do not acknowledge the contributions of Afrikan Americans to the advancement of science and technology or the contributions of Afrikan civilizations to the rest of the world. This is an act of omission.

Commission/omission reinforces the false notion of European superiority and the equally false notion of Afrikan inferiority. The continuous infusion of primary research is important to the development and implementation of a balanced and intellectually sound curriculum. An Afrikan-centered education provides an opportunity for a more equitable picture of information about the world. Such an approach will have an impact on all students within the district.

INDABA PRINCIPLE SIX: DECONSTRUCTION

The process used to identify persons, ideas, and institutions responsible for the deliberate construction, glorification, and elevation of European culture and history to the detriment of Afrikans as well as other non-European groups is referred to as *Deconstruction*. In the past, school systems have often included information about African Americans in segments, or during the month of February, or in one or two modules of learning. These meager inclusions of facts or anecdotes about African Americans are not enough. In this scenario, an Afrikan-centered philosophy is the very framework for education itself. Such a philosophy means that administrators and school boards must be bold in raising fundamental questions about the nature of the Eurocentric enterprise in a multicultural society, and particularly in an overwhelmingly African American school district.

The idea of European hegemony in education is incorrect and cannot continue to be promoted as the only correct view. None of these ideas will have a full impact on education until there are changes in university schools of education. It is still possible for a teacher who will eventually teach in an urban setting to complete a degree without taking a course that will prepare him/her to interact positively and with sensitivity with non-European cultures. By pointing to other perspectives, including Native Americans, Asians, and Latino as well, African-centered education suggests a pluralism without hierarchy. This means that the Eurocentric idea will not control the structure of knowledge but become, as it should have been all along, one perspective among many.

INDABA PRINCIPLE SEVEN: RECONSTRUCTION/ SELF-DETERMINATION

Reconstruction/Self-Determination is the process of developing critical and creative thinking through the acquisition and analysis of the historical experiences of one's own group. Children who fail to know their own history and culture are apt to believe that their history and culture are of secondary importance at best. The best way to tap the creativity and intelligence of a child is to center the child first in his/her own historical and cultural experience. Respect for others is achieved as a result of respect for "self." Afrikan-centered education is intended to strengthen Afrikan children's self-concept and have them view their Afrikaness with pride and dignity instead of disdain and humiliation. Although the primary objective of an Afrikan-centered education is not primarily to increase self-esteem, increased self-esteem is a positive outcome.

Reconstruction/Self-Determination is the ability to define, develop, defend, create, and control the destiny of self, family, community, and nation. Afrikan-centered principles can be applied to children of all cultures. When children find pride within themselves and their culture, children will achieve what they believe.

CRITERIA FOR SELECTING TEXTBOOKS AND OTHER LEARNING MATERIAL

This criteria was developed by Detroit Public Schools using the principles of MA'AT, i.e. *truth, balance, order,* and *harmony*. Using the criteria, school districts can let textbook publishers know what is and is not acceptable as learning materials for the school district. The days when school districts spent millions of dollars on outdated racist material are long gone. The following are good not only for school districts, but also for helping parents determine learning materials that are good for their children at home and school.

—Kwame Kenyatta

Textbooks and learning materials selected for use will meet or exceed the quality standards currently used in the textbook selection process and the additional criteria listed below.

1. CONTENT AND LEARNING MATERIALS WILL BE SCREENED FOR *TRUTH* AS DEFINED BY

- content that can be documented and defended using primary sources wherever possible,

- the availability of bibliographies and other source materials,

- inclusiveness of content that is known and documented but traditionally omitted through negligence or design,

- content that is free of distortions such as misrepresentations, oversimplifications, and erroneous attributions and conclusions,

- the use of photographs instead of artist's renderings whenever possible,

- charts, diagrams, photographs, illustrations, and side bars that enhance content and support truth,

- maps that show proportional landmass and explain the difference between natural and political geography, such as Peter's Projection maps, and

- authors and contributors with extensive knowledge/credentials and experience in the field and proven sensitivity to the group or subject involved.

2. CONTENT AND LEARNING MATERIALS WILL BE SCREENED FOR BALANCE, MEANING THAT THE MATERIAL WILL BE

- infused with the concepts underlying multiculturalism such as the oneness of humanity and the inter-dependence and interrelation of cultural and ethnic groups,

- free of excesses, extremes, exaggerations, incomplete thoughts, and half-truths,

- reflective of different viewpoints that encourage and foster critical thinking,

- reflective of diverse instructional strategies, and

- contextually balanced with regard to illustrations and portrayals of various cultural and ethnic groups.

3. CONTENT AND LEARNING MATERIALS WILL BE SCREENED FOR ORDER AND HAVE

- historical order and sequence that reflect the universal development of cultures and ethnic groups,

- parallel chronological events reported in perspective,

- topics and concepts treated in sufficient depth to enhance understanding, and

- examples that are relevant, meaningful to the given curriculum content, and illustrative of principles, generalizations, and theories.

4. CONTENT AND LEARNING MATERIALS WILL BE SCREENED FOR HARMONY IN THAT

- words, names, and views used are the same as those used by the subject group; that is, call people what they call themselves,

- positive, human events are used as historical and/or relevant guideposts,

- materials are written from the perspective of the group(s) being discussed, and

- there is inclusion of various perspectives and significant examples of folklore, customs, symbols, and practices related to the topics.

5. CONTENT AND LEARNING MATERIALS MUST BE BIAS-FREE AND MULTICULTURAL IN THAT THERE IS

- no overrepresentation,

- no underrepresentation,

- no stereotyping,

- no glossing over of issues,

- no deliberate isolation and fragmentation,

- no discriminatory language,

- no marginalizing of contributions, and

- no evidence of propaganda or hidden purpose.

DETROIT PUBLIC SCHOOLS AFRIKAN-CENTERED EDUCATION STRANDS

The ***Detroit Public School Core Curriculum for Social Studies*** is used as the framework for infusing Afrikan-centered education throughout the district. The following strands were designed to develop positive self-concept in our students while emphasizing values and culture. The Afrikan-centered strands presented here can be implemented in any school district. This ***Core Curriculum*** will empower our students with a sense of identity, purpose, and direction, moving them toward a self-determining future.

Pre-Kindergarten through Grade 4

SOCIAL STUDIES SCOPE AND SEQUENCE	AFRIKAN-CENTERED EDUCATION OUTCOMES AND OBJECTIVES
PK-K:	Develop a positive self-concept, emphazing values, ethnic background, and culture as reflected in the principles of unity, self-determination, collective work and responsibility, cooperative economics, purpose, creativity, and faith.
Myself and Others	～ Identify self.
	～ Recognize the importance of one's name to one's identity.
	～ Define a family and name ways in which different families celebrate different holidays.

Source: *Social Studies Core Curriculum Outcomes and Objectives: Pre-Kindergarten—Grade 12 Curriculum Document*, Prepared by the Office of Social Studies, Detroit Public Schools, Copyrighted June 1994.

SOCIAL STUDIES SCOPE AND SEQUENCE	AFRIKAN-CENTERED EDUCATION OUTCOMES AND OBJECTIVES
Grade 1: School and Family	Develop a positive self-concept, emphazing self-worth, values, ethnic background, and culture as reflected in the principles of unity, self-determination, collective work and responsibility, cooperative economics, purpose, creativity, and faith. ↝ Describe the importance of the family as a basic unit of society. ↝ Identify examples of positive concepts involving families. ↝ Compare and contrast the family unit in Afrika and America.
Grade 2: Neighborhoods	Develop a positive self-concept about neighborhood, emphasizing self-worth, values, ethnic background, and culture as reflected in the principles of unity, self-determination, collective work and responsibility, cooperative economics, purpose, creativity, and faith. ↝ Compare and contrast the concept of village life in Afrika with the concept of neighborhoods in the United States.
Grade 3: Communities/ Detroit	Understand the importance of cultural transmission. ↝ Identify elements in Afrikan American culture retained from Afrikan origins. ↝ Describe ways in which folktales, music, dance, and art define the culture. ↝ Describe and analyze Paradise Valley as a model of a cultural community within an urban environment.
Grade 4: Regions/ Michigan	Analyze the dispersion of Afrikan Americans throughout regions. ↝ Design bar graphs to illustrate the dispersion of African Americans throughout various regions. ↝ Identify African American historical sites in Michigan and other regions.

Source: *Social Studies Core Curriculum Outcomes and Objectives: Pre-Kindergarten—Grade 12 Curriculum Document*, Prepared by the Office of Social Studies, Detroit Public Schools, Copyrighted June 1994.

SOCIAL STUDIES SCOPE AND SEQUENCE	AFRIKAN-CENTERED EDUCATION OUTCOMES AND OBJECTIVES

Grade 5:
 	
American History
	Evaluate the impact of Afrikans and Afrikans Americans on the development of North America.
	
	~ Research, describe, and discuss the roles of Afrikans and Afrikan Americans in the following eras:
	  ■ pre-European colonization of North America
	  ■ enslavement of Afrikans
	  ■ legalization of slavery and the development of a slave culture
	  ■ wars
	  ■ Reconstruction
	  ■ post-Reconstruction
	  ■ Harlem Renaissance
	  ■ segregation and desegregation
	  ■ Civil Rights struggles
	
	Recognize the existence of Afrikan American entrepreneurs and inventors throughout the history of the United States.
	
	~ Sequence and explain Afrikan American entrepreneurship, in context, in the development of the United States.

Grade 6: Survey of the Social Sciences	**Understand the Principles of *Nguzo Saba*: *Umoja* (Unity), *Kujichagulia* (Self-Determination), *Ujima* (Collective Work and Responsibility), *Ujamaa* (Cooperative Economics), *Nia* (Purpose), *Kuumba* (Creativity), *Imani* (Faith).** ~ Identify the behaviors associated with the principles of Nguzo Saba. ~ Organize a small business plan and seek financial resources.

Source: *Social Studies Core Curriculum Outcomes and Objectives: Pre-Kindergarten—Grade 12 Curriculum Document*, Prepared by the Office of Social Studies, Detroit Public Schools, Copyrighted June 1994.

Grade 7 through Grade 8

SOCIAL STUDIES SCOPE AND SEQUENCE	AFRIKAN-CENTERED EDUCATION OUTCOMES AND OBJECTIVES
Grade 7: World Geography	**Use the geographic themes of location, place, human/environment relations, movement, and regions related to major Afrikan countries.** ~ Explain that human life originated in Afrika. ~ Describe how Afrikan migration patterns impacted the world. ~ Identify climatic regions of Afrika. ~ Identify valuable resources of Afrika and explain how they contributed to the colonization and exploitation of the continent.
Grade 8: United States History to 1865	**Assess how Afrikan Americans contributed to the historical development of the United States through the Civil War.** ~ Describe precolonial and colonial Afrikan American influences in the Americas. ~ Evaluate the impact of early American governmental foundations on Afrikan Americans. ~ Analyze how Afrikan Americans were affected by political decisions and policies before the Civil War. ~ Explain the role of Afrikan American contributions in wartime. **Understand the impact of Afrikan Americans in the development of the economic system of the United States.** ~ Analyze and discuss the economic impact of Triangular Trade. ~ Apply the fundamenttal concepts of economics to the institution of slavery and assess its impact on the growth and development of the country.

Source: *Social Studies Core Curriculum Outcomes and Objectives: Pre-Kindergarten—Grade 12 Curriculum Document*, Prepared by the Office of Social Studies, Detroit Public Schools, Copyrighted June 1994.

High School Level

SOCIAL STUDIES SCOPE AND SEQUENCE	AFRIKAN-CENTERED EDUCATION OUTCOMES AND OBJECTIVES
Year 1: United States History Since 1865	**Understand the role of the Afrikans and Afrikan Americans in historical events as they relate to U.S. History since the Civil War.** 🙰 Analyze the impact of slavery/racism on the historical, educational, and economic development of the Afrikan American community. **Understand the concepts of *Ujima* and *Ujamaa* as they relate to the economic history of Afrikan Americans.** 🙰 Define the concepts of *Ujima* and *Ujamaa* and relate them historically to the development of Black businesses prior to 1954. 🙰 Analyze how the concept of integration destroyed Black entrepreneurship after that date, and investigate the efforts of the present day community to revitalize the areas in which the reside. **Understand how Afrikan Americans have developed technological innovations and inventions in the United States since the Civil War.** 🙰 List and report on examples of Afrikan American inventions and innovations, in context, as well as their development and use in modern life.
Year 2: Global Issues	**Trace the migration of humankind from its Afrikan origins.** 🙰 Contruct a time line identifying dispersion of humankind from the Afrikan continent. 🙰 Explain the cause-and-effect relationship between external invasions and internal migrations in Afrika.

Source: *Social Studies Core Curriculum Outcomes and Objectives: Pre-Kindergarten—Grade 12 Curriculum Document*, Prepared by the Office of Social Studies, Detroit Public Schools, Copyrighted June 1994.

High School Level

SOCIAL STUDIES SCOPE AND SEQUENCE	AFRIKAN-CENTERED EDUCATION OUTCOMES AND OBJECTIVES
Year 2: Geography	**Analyze the Afrikan Diaspora and its effects on the Afrikan continent and the rest of the world.** 〜 Interpret the relationship and impact of land features, climate, and natural resources on the economy and movement of people. 〜 Appraise the impact of colonization on the underdevelopment of the Afrikan continent.
Year 3: Government	**Analyze the role of Afrikan Americans in local, state, and national governments.** 〜 Trace the evolution of Afrikan American political power and its effect on local, state and national affairs and government.
Year 3: Economics	**Analyze and apply cooperative economics and collective work and responsibility:** 〜 Design models to illustrate how cooperative economics could be used in the Afrikan American community and nation. 〜 Identify prominent Afrikan American businesses and business leaders in the local community and surrounding areas. 〜 Identify the impact on the Afrikan American community of economic practices used by other groups.

Source: *Social Studies Core Curriculum Outcomes and Objectives: Pre-Kindergarten—Grade 12 Curriculum Document*, Prepared by the Office of Social Studies, Detroit Public Schools, Copyrighted June 1994.

IN CELEBRATION OF BLACK HOLY DAYS

The **Black Holy Days** and the **Harambee Circle** are presented here to provide educators and parents with Afrikan-centered ceremonies and celebrations. These holidays can be celebrated in school and at home, providing fun and learning at the same time. The **Harambee Circle** can be performed in elementary and middle schools at the beginning and/or end of each day. Both the celebration of **Black Holy Days** and the **Harambee Circle** provide students with a sense of identity, purpose, and direction.

MARTIN LUTHER KING, JR., DAY   JANUARY 15
A day to celebrate the life and contributions of Martin Luther King, Jr.

BLACK HISTORY MONTH   FEBRUARY
A month-long celebration of the contributions of Afrikan people to civilization

BLACK NATION DAY   MARCH 29
A day to celebrate the founding of the modern-day new Afrikan nation

MALCOLM X DAY   MAY 19
A day to celebrate the life and contributions of Malcolm X

▲ Dancing in the street—A celebration of culture

▲ I have a Dream
Martin Luther King, Jr.
January 15, 1929—April 4, 1968

▲ Freedom by any means necessary
Malcolm X
May 19, 1925—February 21, 1965

▲ Up you mighty race!   Marcus Garvey

AFRIKAN LIBERATION DAY   MAY 25

ALD is a day to show support for the worldwide Afrikan Liberation Movement.

MARCUS GARVEY DAY   AUGUST 17

A celebration of the life and contributions of Marcus Garvey

BLACK READING MONTH   SEPTEMBER

A time to promote the reading of literature written by and for people of Afrikan descent.

AFRIKAN HOLOCAUST DAY   OCTOBER 12

A day to commemorate the millions of Afrikans who died at the hands of the Europeans from the west.

ANCESTORS DAY   OCTOBER 31

A day to dressup as our ancestors and celebrate their memory with games, music, food, etc.

KWANZAA   DECEMBER 26

A seven day celebration of Afrikan and new Afrikan culture nation.

SUGGESTED CLASSROOM ACTIVITIES IN CELEBRATION OF MALCOLM X DAY

Discuss basic facts about Malcolm X's life, his family, his activities, and his role in history.

When and why did Malcolm Little change his name to Malcolm X and later to El Hajj Malik El Shabazz?

Have students read selected speeches or letters of Malcolm X. Using these selections, assist students in writing a statement of their own which they feel summarizes Malcolm X's ideas.

Have students read the Declaration of Independence and the Preamble to the Constitution to find some rights of citizens Malcolm X was working to achieve.

Speculate on what Malcolm X might be doing had he lived.

Have students write reports comparing the lives of Martin Luther King, Jr. and Malcolm X. Specific questions to consider: What goals did they share? How did their philosophies differ?

USE THE FOLLOWING QUOTES FROM MALCOLM X FOR CLASS DISCUSSION OR AS A WRITING ASSIGNMENTS

"Every effort we make to unite among ourselves on the basis of what we are, they label it as what? Racism. This is the 'racism' trap."

"You can't have a positive attitude toward yourself and a negative attitude toward Africa at the same time. To the same degree that your understanding of and attitude toward Africa become positive, you'll find that your attitude and your understanding of yourself will become positive."

"A better understanding of the past helps you to understand the present and be better prepared for the future."

"Education is our passport to the future, for tomorrow belongs to the people who prepare for it today."

"One of the first things I think young people, especially nowadays, should learn how to do is see for yourself and listen for yourself and think for yourself. Then you can come to an intellegent decision for yourself."

SUGGESTED HARAMBEE CIRCLE

LIFT EVERY VOICE AND SING

By James Weldon Johnson

Lift every voice and sing, Till earth and heaven ring,
Ring with the harmonies of liberty;
Let our rejoicing rise High as the listening skies,
Let it resound loud as the rolling sea.
Sing a song full of the faith that the dark past has taught us;
Sing a song full of the hope that the present has brought us;
Facing the rising sun of our new day begun,
Let us march on til victory is won.

NGUZO SABA (SEVEN PRINCIPLES) SONG
(Leader) We Got **UMOJA**
(Student) We Got **UMOJA**
(Leader) And That's **UNITY**
(Student) And That's **UNITY**

(repeat in same manner until all principles are sung)

KUJICHAGULIA	SELF-DETERMINATION
UJIMA	COLLECTIVE WORK AND RESPONSIBILITY
UJAMAA	COOPERATIVE ECONOMICS
NIA	PURPOSE
KUUMBA	CREATIVITY
IMANI	FAITH

COLORS RED, BLACK, & GREEN

RED—Stands for the blood that black people have shed, are shedding, and will continue to shed for the liberation of Afrikan people.

BLACK—Stands for the first principle , UMOJA. We are Afrikan people.

GREEN—Stands for the fertility of our Motherland; we shall fight to set her free.

"I AM SOMEBODY"

I am SOMEBODY
I may not look like EVERYBODY,
But I am SOMEBODY
I feel like I am SOMEBODY.
I look like I am SOMEBODY.
I act like I am SOMEBODY.
EVERYBODY is SOMEBODY to SOMEBODY.
NOBODY but NOBODY can make me feel like a NOBODY.
"If you want to love SOMEBODY, then love ME".
"If you want to help Somebody, then help ME".
"I AM SOMEBODY. And don't you ever forget it!"

IF YOU'RE AFRIKAN AND YOU KNOW IT (SONG)
(to the tune of "If You're Happy and You Know It")

If you're Afrikan and you know it clap your hands (repeat twice)
If you're Afrikan and you know it, and you're not too proud to show it,
If you're Afrikan and you know it clap your hands.

If you're Afrikan and you know it stomp your feet (repeat twice)
If you're Afrikan and you know it, and you're not too proud to show it,
If you're Afrikan and you know it stomp your feet.

If you're Afrikan and you know it shake your head (repeat twice)
If you're Afrikan and you know it, and you're too proud to show it,
If you're Afrikan and you know it shake your head.

If you're Afrikan and you know it say Yebo (repeat twice)
If you're Afrikan and you know it, and you're not too proud to show it,
If you're Afrikan and you know it say Yebo.

Harambee Harambee Harambee Harambee Harambee Harambee Harambee

AFRIKAN-CENTERED CHARTS

The following three charts provide an understanding of three important subjects. The first chart is the Afrikan-centered value system. It highlights the traditional value system practiced by Afrikan people thousands of years ago using the principles of **MA'AT** as its base. The second chart is a Eurocentric value system chart highlighting the traditonal value system practiced by Europeans for thousands of years, based on the myth of white supremacy. The third chart is the use of the **Nguzo Saba** principles and shows how they can be used in school and at home to produce a balanced Afrikan personality and perspective.

—*Kwame Kenyatta*

Chart #1

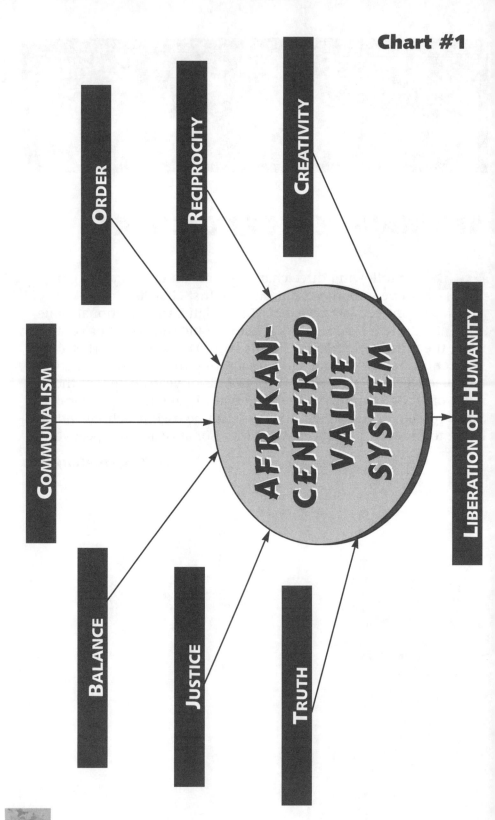

Chart #2

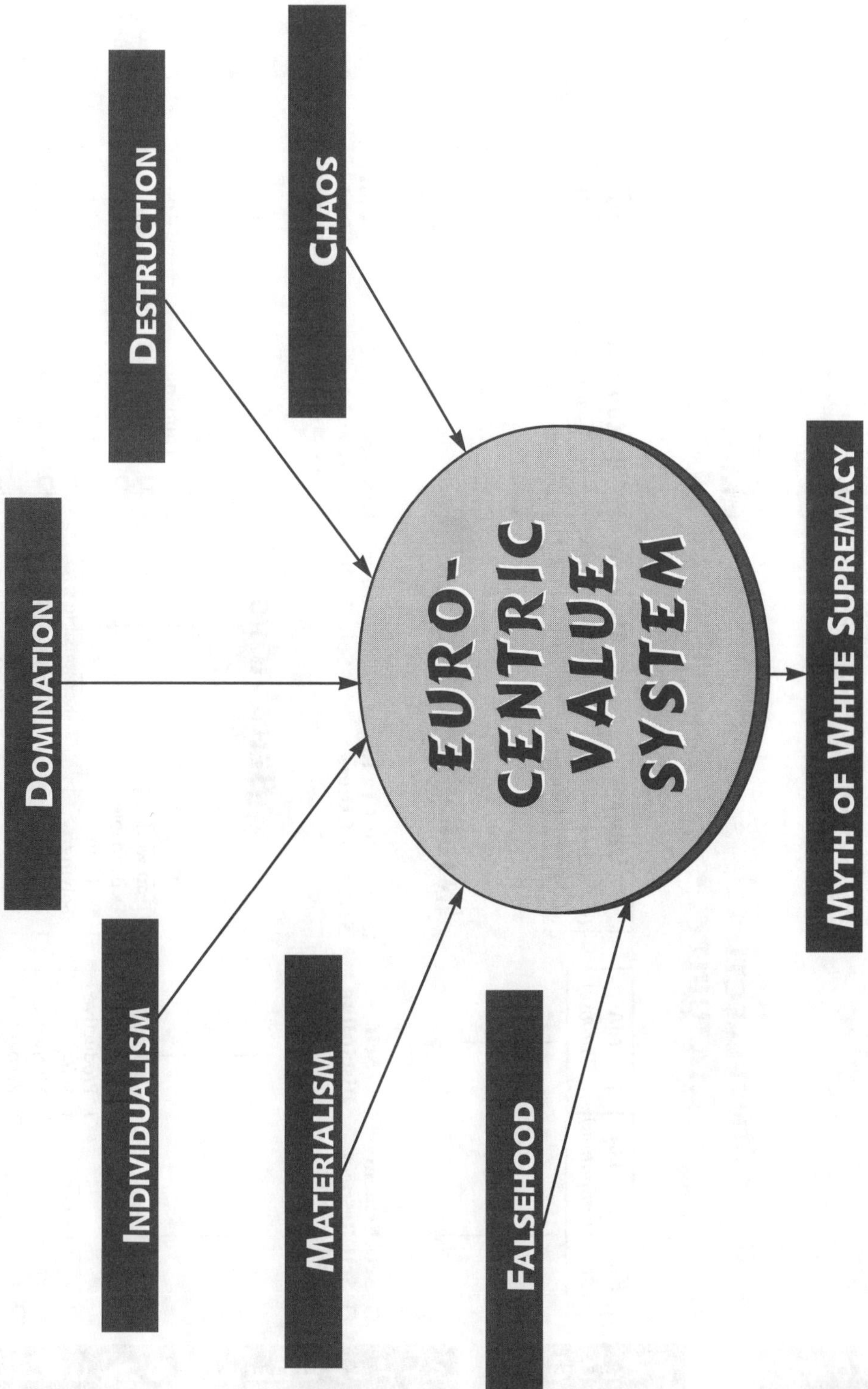

DESTRUCTION

CHAOS

DOMINATION

INDIVIDUALISM

MATERIALISM

FALSEHOOD

EURO-CENTRIC VALUE SYSTEM

MYTH OF WHITE SUPREMACY

Chart #3: Nguzo Saba Principles

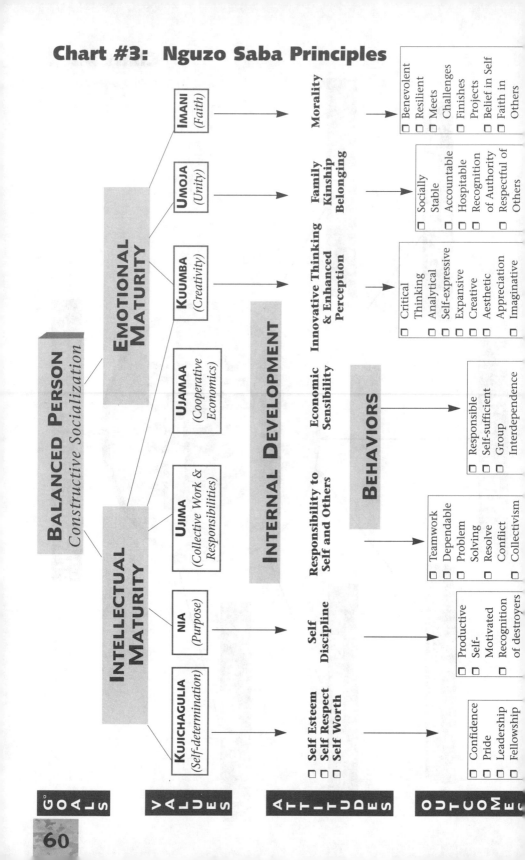

GOALS

BALANCED PERSON
Constructive Socialization

EMOTIONAL MATURITY

INTELLECTUAL MATURITY

VALUES

| KUJICHAGULIA *(Self-determination)* | NIA *(Purpose)* | UJIMA *(Collective Work & Responsibilities)* | UJAMAA *(Cooperative Economics)* | KUUMBA *(Creativity)* | UMOJA *(Unity)* | IMANI *(Faith)* |

INTERNAL DEVELOPMENT

ATTITUDES

| Self Esteem Self Respect Self Worth | Self Discipline | Responsibility to Self and Others | Economic Sensibility | Innovative Thinking & Enhanced Perception | Family Kinship Belonging | Morality |

BEHAVIORS

OUTCOME

Self Esteem, Self Respect, Self Worth →
- ☐ Confidence
- ☐ Pride
- ☐ Leadership
- ☐ Fellowship

Self Discipline →
- ☐ Productive
- ☐ Self-Motivated
- ☐ Recognition of destroyers

Responsibility to Self and Others →
- ☐ Teamwork
- ☐ Dependable
- ☐ Problem Solving
- ☐ Resolve Conflict
- ☐ Collectivism

Economic Sensibility →
- ☐ Responsible
- ☐ Self-sufficient
- ☐ Group Interdependence

Innovative Thinking & Enhanced Perception →
- ☐ Critical Thinking
- ☐ Analytical
- ☐ Self-expressive
- ☐ Expansive
- ☐ Creative
- ☐ Aesthetic Appreciation
- ☐ Imaginative

Family Kinship Belonging →
- ☐ Socially Stable
- ☐ Accountable
- ☐ Hospitable
- ☐ Recognition of Authority
- ☐ Respectful of Others

Morality →
- ☐ Benevolent
- ☐ Resilient
- ☐ Meets Challenges
- ☐ Finishes Projects
- ☐ Belief in Self
- ☐ Faith in Others

60

SUGGESTED READING LIST

The following suggested reading list is provided for educators, parents, and students, and can be found at your local Black bookstore and the local library.

—Kwame Kenyatta

YOUNG ADULT TITLES

Your History	J.A. Rogers
Spider Anasy	James Berry
The Boy Who Did Not Believe in Spring	Lucille Clifton
The Day They Stole the Letter J	Jabari Mahiri
The Tiger Who Wore White Gloves	Gwendolyn Brooks
Why Mosquitoes Buss	Verba Aardema
Why the Creab Has No Head	Barnara Knutson
Tales of Ashanti Father	Peggy Appiah
John Henry	Ezra Jack Keats
Malcolm X	Arnold Adoff
Martin Luther King Jr. (Troll)	Rae Bains
Moja Means One	Muriel/Tom Feelings
Now Sheba Sings the Song	Maya Angelou
Oh Kojo! How Could You	Verna Aardema
Shaka: King of the Zulus	D. Stanley/ P. Vennema
Sundiata, Lion King of Mali	David Wisniewski

POLITICS/HISTORY

The Political Work of Marcus Garvey	Tony Martin
100 Amazing Facts About the Negro	J.A. Rogers
100 Years of Lynching	Ralph Ginsburg
Bad Blood	James H. Jones
Destruction of Black Civilization	Chancellor Williams
Five Negro Presidents	J.A. Rogers
From Babylon to Timbuktu	Rudolph Windsor
From Columbus to Castro	Dr. Eric Williams
From Superman to Man	J.A. Rogers
History of Negro People in the US Vol. I	Herbert Apthker
History of Negro People in the US Vol. II	Herbert Apthker
1910-1932	
How Europe Underdeveloped Africa	Walter Rodney
Ku Klux Spirit	J.A. Rogers
Malcolm X Last Speeches	Eric Man
Maurice Bishop Speaks	Steve Clark

The African Origin of Civilization	Cheikh Anta Diop
Myth or Reality	
They Came Before Columbus	Ivan Van Seritma
They Stole It, But You Must Return It	Dr. Richard Williams
Valley of Dry Bones	Rudolph Windsor
World and Afrika	W.E.B. Du Bois

PSYCHOLOGY

Black Skin White Masks	Frantz Fanon
Chains & Images of Psychological Slavery	Dr. Naim Akbar
From the Browder File	Anthony T. Browder
Psychopathic Racial Personality	Bobby E. Wright
Fall of America	Elijah Muhammed

PSYCHOLOGY/PHILOSOPHY

Black Bourgeoisie	E. Franklin Frazier
Black Consciousness	Steve Biko
Black Masculinity	Robert Staples
Bringing the Black Boy to Manhood	Nathan Hare
Community to Self	Dr. Naim Akbar
Conspiracy to Destroy Black Boys (Vol. I-II)	Dr. Jawanza Kunjufu
Crisis of the Negro Intellectual	Harold Cruise
Developing Positive Self Images	Dr. Jawanza Kunjufu
Developmental Psychology of Black Child	A. Wilson
Jambalaya: Natural Woman's Book	Luisah Teish
Message to the Black Man	Hon. Elijah Muhammad
Miseducation of the Negro	Carter G. Woodson
Motivating-Preparing Black Youth to Work	Dr. Jawanza Kunjufu
Racial Matters	Martin Luther King, Jr.
Rasta & Resistance	Horace Campbell
Sex & Race (Vol. I-III)	J.A. Rogers
Up From Slavery	Booker T. Washington

LITERATURE

Slave Girl	Linda Brent
The Souls of Black Folks	W.E.B. Du Bois
The Spook Who Sat by the Door	Sam Green Lee
Their Eyes Were Watching God	Zora Neale Hurston
When and Where I Enter	Paula Guddings
Black Boy	Richard Wright
Black Women in White America	Gerda Lerner
Native Son	Richard Wright
New Black Voices	Chapman
The Middle Passage White Ships & Black Cargo	Tom Feelings
African American Folk tales For Young Readers	

HISTORY

Africa Must Unite	Kwame Nkrumah
African Glory	J.C. De Graft
African Origin of Civilization	Cheikh Anta Diop
African Presence in Early American	Ivan Van Sertima
African Presence in Early Asia	Ivan Van Sertima
African Presence in Early Europe	Ivan Van Sertima
Africa's Gift to America	J.A. Rogers
Africa: Mother of Western Civilization	Yosef Ben-Jochanan

SUGGESTED READING LIST (cont'd...)

Afrocentricity	Molefi Kete Asante
Classic Africa	Molefi Kete Asante
African American Biography (Vol. I-IV)	
African American History:	
A Journey of Liberation	Molefi Kete Asante
Assassination of Malcolm X	Breitman, Porter Smith
Before the Mayflower	Lerone Bennet
Black Africa	Cheikh Anta Diop
Blacks in Science	Ivan Van Sertima
Black Indians	William Loren Katz
Black Man of the Nile	Yosef Ben-Jochanan
Black Women in Antiquity	Ivan Van Sertima
Blacks in America's Wat	Robert Mullen
Ethiopia the Origin of Civilization	John G. Jackson
Introduction to African Civilization	John G. Jackson
Life & Times of Frederick Douglass	Frederick Douglass
Negro in the Making of America	Benjamin Quarles
Nile Valley Civilization	Ivan Van Sertima
1999 Facts About Blacks	Raymond M. Corgin
Revolutionary Path	Kwame Nkrumah
Stolen Legacy	George G.M. James
Wretched of the Earth	Frantz Fanon

RELIGION

Ancient Egyptian Religion	Henri Frankford
Book of the Dead	E.A. Budge
Christianity Before Christ	John Jackson
Flash of Spirit	Robert Harris Thompson
Lost Books of the Bible	
Man, God and Civilization	John C. Jackson
Negro Church in America	C. Eric Lincoln
The Black Messiah	Albert B. Cleage, Jr.
What Color Was Jesus?	William Mosley
What Color is Your God?	Sally Ann Behm

BIOGRAPHY

Angela Davis: Autobiography	Angela Davis
Assata	Assata Shakur
Autobiography of W.E.B. Du Bois	Dr. Herbert Apptheker
Black Inventors of America	Burt McKinley Jr.
Black Robes, White Justice	Bruce Wright
Bloods	Wallace Terry
Brothers	Sylvester Monroe & Peter Goldman
By Any Means Necessary	Malcolm X
Frederick Douglass Writings (5 Vols.)	F. Douglass
Golden Names for Afrikan People	Mia Damali
Great Afrikan Thinkers	Ivan Van Sertima
Great Black Leaders	Ivan Van Sertima
World's Great Men of Colour (Vol I-II)	J.A. Rogers
Paul Robeson Speaks	Philip Foner
Autobiography of Malcolm X	Alex Haley
The Last Year of Malcolm X	Bruce Perry
Two Speeches by Malcolm X	

SUGGESTED READING LIST (cont'd...)

CULTURE
Kwanzaa   Cedric McClester

SPORTS
K.A. System of Karate   Al Mu Assis Karriem

SCHOLAR'S LIBRARIES
The Maroon Within Us   Asa G. Hilliard
Afrocentricity   Molefi Kete Asante
Kemet, Afrocentricity and Knowledge   Molefi Kete Asante
10 Great African American Men of Science
With Hands on Science Activities   Dr. Clifford Watson, Principal
                                                Malcolm X Academy, Detroit, MI

CONCLUSION

—Joann Watson

frikan-centered education in the public school is an holistic, healthy, and healing process that appropriately *centers* the first human beings and the elements of the earliest civilization within a historically correct framework that is affirming, inclusive, and empirically sound.

Because of the very nature of public schools, deliberation and discussion may emerge around Afrikan-centeredness that could trigger debates about the perceived need to authenticate or validate Afrikan-centeredness by persons or institutions who are ill-equipped, ill-advised, and ill-suited for the task.

In some communities there may also be forces who appear to be of Afrikan descent but who are not Afrikan-rooted and who will publicly oppose, denigrate and denounce the value, worth, and importance of Afrikan-centered education.

Any such betrayal of the Afrikan-centered education should be utilized as a "teaching opportunity" by the Council of Elders, Pan-Afrikanist, Nationalist, and the conscious community to exemplify the betrayers' conduct as the evidence of great need, with concurrent organizing education of the masses via print and electronic media which is under the auspices of Afrikan ownership.

Afrikan-centered education should not be marginalized, trivialized, downsized, tranquilized, or homogenized to ease the comfort zone of non-Afrikans or to satisfy the internalized oppression (self-hatred) of these Afrikans who may have appointed themselves as deniers of the Afrikan Holocaust and apologists for European oppressors.

Under no circumstances should educators of any background who display levels of discomfort or intolerance with the Afrikan-centered philosophy be designated as instructors. Researchers have clearly documented a demonstrable surge among students who display a love of learning, a love of self, a love for others, and a heightened sense of respect and dignity for all.

Afrikan-centered education is truly an "ACE" for cleansing, filtering, and reversing dangerous and deliberating dogmas which have too long been tools of destruction among Afrikan people. Mainstream Afrikan-centered education provides appropriate school reform methodology within and among public schools throughout America which face enormous challenges on the threshold of the twenty-first century and beyond.

BIOGRAPHICAL SKETCH OF KWAME KENYATTA

Kwame Kenyatta is a former Vice-President of the Detroit Board of Education. He served on the board from November 1992 until November 1997.

Mr. Kenyatta has a long history of struggle and commitment to healing the Black community and uplifting the Afrikan personality. He is the former Coordinator of the Detroit Chapter of the New Afrikan People's Organization and the Malcolm X Grass-roots Movement. Also, he is cofounder of Afrikan Way Investment and National Coordinator of Fihankra International.

Due in large part to his reputation and dedication to his community, Mr. Kenyatta has appeared on both local and national television and radio programs including: *Night Talk with Bob Law*, *The Sally Jessie Raphael Show*, *The Jerry Springer Show*, and ABC's *Nightline*. He has been interviewed by many major daily and weekly newspapers in the country.

During his five years on the board, Mr. Kenyatta has provided innovative idea and programs. He is a proponent of Afrikan-centered education and believes that it lays the foundation for new and progressive learning styles in education. Further, he believes that the way to build or rebuild the Afrikan personality is to instill a strong concept of identity, purpose, and direction rooted in the New Afrikan value system known as the Nguzo Saba.

As a cultural consultant, Mr. Kenyatta has conducted Afrikan Naming Ceremonies, Afrikan weddings, Manhood Training, Kwanzaa

Programs, Afrikan History Lectures, and a host of other programs. He is also preparing to publish a collection of his speeches, essays, poems and political thoughts entitled *Burning Fire: An Afrikan-Centered Worldview.*

Although Kwame Kenyatta is respected and supported by thousands, he views himself as a "plain and simple brother" trying to do something for his people.

KWAME KENYATTA IS AVAILABLE FOR SPEAKING ENGAGEMENTS, CONFERENCES, AND WORKSHOPS. (313) 835-7981

APPENDICES

APPENDIX A
The Last Child

Dr. Kay Lovelace

APPENDIX B
Background on Detroit's Afrikan-Centered Male/Female Academies

Clifford Watson, Ed.D.

APPENDIX C
A Word About Afrikan-Centered Education

Malik Yakini

THE LAST CHILD

Dr. Kay Lovelace Ed.
Former Executive Director
Professional Development and Technology
Detroit Public Schools

With the concept of integration looming in the forefront in the early 1960s, proponents of an equitable education pushed for the inclusion of "black studies." The intent, as it is today, was to correct the inaccurate accounts of the contributions of African Americans in the development of the United States and to pursue for the contributors their rightful place in the annals of history. An attempt to broaden this perspective resulted in a sensitivity to the misrepresentation of additional cultures in addition to African Americans in historical accounts, and "Department of Black Studies" was soon consumed almost completely by the "Department of Ethnic Studies" across the country.

The teaching of *Black Studies* in the 60s and 70s was certainly not a new concept. Beginning with reconstruction in the South in 1868, black delegates took part in government for the first time by voting in new state constitutions that made significant and creative contributions that led to the successful revitalization of the South. Black history was taught with diligence, accuracy, and pride. Black colleges, an outgrowth of this period, provided educational institutions for the "Negro" student, but were also places where history was recorded and taught with the intention of giving students a foundation for the endless career choices that supposedly would be available to them.

The inclusion of the negro in the American dream appeared to be only a matter of time, but that time never came. Dr. Martin Luther

▲ Kay Lovelace

King, Jr. commented during his Centennial Address in 1968: "...The documentation of the negro in the rebuilding of the South would be altered forever by white propagandists, the myth-makers of negro history. In this altercation, negroes were ignorant, evil, stupid, incapable of handling freedom. Generations of Americans were assiduously taught this falsehood and the collective mind of America became poisoned with racism and stunted with myths."

It is now near the turn of the century and multiculturalism has replaced "ethnic studies." Out of curiosity, one must ask why it is that when Afrikan American Studies (alias "black studies") is introduced, multiculturalism (alias "ethnic studies") is introduced? Perhaps first we need to ask what is meant by *multiculturalism*? At face value, multiculturalism in its present form might be the inclusion of all cultures and their unique contribution to the development of past and present civilizations.

Multiculturalism is intended, then, to represent several individual cultures —not all cultures, but several *individual* cultures. The task now becomes to identify *which* individual cultures we are referring to when we use the term *multicultural*. Would the several individual cultures be the same across the country? Would they change depending on, say, the southwest versus the northwest? Or would they be the cultures whose population make up the greatest percentages of the total populations of this country? Herein lies a dilemma, for our educational institutions have issued several poetic proclamations demanding equitable education for all students. Just *who* are we referring to when we say *all*?

Unlike *multiculturalism*, which suggests inclusion, the term *all* indicates that some students have been left out in previous educational agendas. Now we say emphatically that "we want to educate *all* students," as if in the past we never intended to educate *all* students. So we will educate all of the students by putting in place a multicultural curriculum designed to honor the unique contributions of the cultures represented. This is a laudable task and one that certainly deserves attention, however, educational institutions now face a second dilemma—not only must they determine which of the several individual cultures they will address in a *multicultural* curriculum; they must also locate accurate information about the contributions of the several individual cultures, particularly those of color, whose history has been so distorted in the major text books and other common and popular publications. How can multiculturalism represent several individual cultures *if the several individual cultures are misrepresented?*

There is nothing wrong with multiculturalism, just as there was nothing wrong with ethnic studies. The fallacy lies in the inclusion of cultures that have not been defined, represented accurately or equitably, and whose ancient historical contributions have been omitted. An accurate history that starts in the year 2,000 B.C. or 3,000 B.C. omits centuries of the glorious beautiful reigns of Afrikan peoples as early as 6,000 B.C. This omission is the pivotal point of difference between an Afrikan-centered curriculum versus a Europeancentered curriculum. *It becomes simply a matter of an accurate account of the beginning of civilization and the people who were influential in the development of that civilization* and as we are finding out, influenced the culture, art, philosophy, architect, sciences, and religions of the world.

Currently, the base of information we have to draw from is inaccurate. Certainly from my viewpoint but more importantly from the research, investigation and empirical study conducted by the world's premier scholars, what we have instead of accuracy in our textbooks, in our curriculum, and in the minds of many national and international populations is a distorted picture showing the myths that have been recorded as *history* since the beginning of European civilizations. We cannot and should not endorse programs or adopt textbooks until we come to a common understanding of what a Ma'at (truthful, ordered, balanced, justified, accurate, righteous) curriculum should be. To design a curriculum and adopt textbooks prior to this process is to defeat the purpose of creating a multicultural curriculum that represents all children and an accurate account of the unique contributions of the individual cultures. The textbooks we select now will not do justice to the balanced curriculum we seek for the future unless we understand Ma'at.

To emphasize this argument, seventy-eight people were asked what they perceived *multiculturalism* to be. Certainly seventy-eight is not a significant number to create empirical research, however for the purposes of this inquiry, their responses were nevertheless intriguing. First, the majority of people did not know what multiculturalism really meant. Second, they did know that it dealt with different ethnic groups. Those named more frequently in the order they were given were Asians, Hispanics, American Indians, Afrikan Americans, Caldeans, and Europeans. Afrikan Americans were seldom mentioned first and in some instances, they were mentioned as an afterthought. I have never known Asians to discuss multicultural-

▲ "I am the black child put me first, not last."

ism. Their interest is on the preservation of their culture, as it is with American Indians, Hispanics and most other cultures.

Where does the need for multiculturalism come from and, more importantly, is it a coincidence that *multiculturalism* surfaced when "Afrikan and Afrikan American studies" began to swell as did "ethnic studies" when "black studies" was in it heyday in the 1960s? The response appears to be that multiculturalism is a genuine attempt to include various cultures. However, without a process within a proper context accepted by all participants, multiculturalism becomes a misunderstood vacuum for people of color that bypasses the painful process of accepting and valuing diverse cultures in its haste to simply include them all. *Multiculturalism* is, in fact, the exact opposite of what people of color are seeking—the correction of distortions, the acknowledgement of the culture's significant scholars and the celebration of the individual culture's contributions. America needs to adopt an agenda that speaks to valuing every child born. In this scenario, we need not identify race, ethnicity, physical and/or mental impairment, or economic status, because every child born is truly valued.

Aside from the need to acknowledge with great reverence the atrocities suffered by the American Indian and the Chinese slave labor force, no other group of people has been so savagely treated as the Afrikan American who was shackled and brought to America and other parts of the "new" world by force under the most inhumane of circumstances. It appears most poignantly, however, when multiculturalism tells of Afrikan American inclusion and the painful story of the need for reciprocity is silenced. If America holds true to her past performance, then might this be the sole purpose of multiculturalism—to continue the misrepresentation of history as did ethnic studies in the 60s? Painfully, once again the Afrikan American child becomes the last child to be considered.

The Afrikan American people or any group of people who find their story distorted or untold must find alternatives to the present multicultural explosion or they will suffer yet another century of exclusion. Educational institutions who intend to educate *all* children must create an environment that celebrates all children based on a thorough correction of distortions, the acknowledgement of the culture's significant scholars and the celebration of the culture's contributions. Just once, I would like to see the Afrikan American child become the first child to be considered because of the devastating circumstances in which he or she has been placed.

An attempt to do this in Detroit resulted in the development of an annual conference called "The Afrikan Child Placed In Crisis." These conferences grew from a mere 700 participants in 1987 to well over 3,000 participants in 1997. While the theme of the conference has changed from year to year, the goals have remained the same—to inform participants about Afrikan and Afrikan American contributions, to provide curriculum models that assist schools in the inclusion of Afrikan and Afrikan American content, to encourage participants to reshape their thinking about Afrikan and Afrikan American contributions and to, thus, provide a base to strengthen the self-concept of Afrikan American children and to inspire participants to include the knowledge gained during the conference in their schools, homes, communities, and within themselves.

The conferences have brought awareness and models of excellence for discussion and consideration. They have created an arena where participants come to celebrate their new knowledge and understanding through conversation, dress and symbolism as they attend approximately five keynote presentations, several special focus sessions and over thirty concurrent workshops. It is the only conference in the country where board members, superintendents, educators, parents, community, business and professional leaders walk side by side to address issues that dramatically impact the education of children of color and poverty. And finally, it has become so popular within the Detroit Public School District that the Detroit Board of Education declared it an institution and opened it to a national audience for its final two years, 1996 and 1997.

Some have said that the title of this conference is demeaning, full of negativism, and that it needs to be changed to something more positive. This may be true; however, this conference is a labor of love that has provided a platform for the recognition of the significance and relevance of sounding the alarm to make everyone aware of what is actually happening to Afrikan American children across this country. When "the enslavement of man by man cease[s] forever" (Frantz Fanon, 1952), then the Afrikan American child will no longer be placed, through no fault of his or her own in circumstances beyond his or her control. And perhaps this child who has endured and survived the most unbelievable odds and too often has been the last to be considered will finally be *first* on our educational agendas.

BACKGROUND ON DETROIT'S AFRIKAN-CENTERED MALE/FEMALE ACADEMIES

Clifford Watson, Ed.D.
Principal
Malcolm X Academy
Detroit Public Schools

The endangered status of Afrikan-American males in this society has become an all-too-familiar topic of discussion. The statistics are well-known and have appeared in popular media as well as scholarly literature. African-American males represent over 50% of the dropouts in urban school systems. They represent over 40% of the Federal prison population. More than any other group, young African American males are most likely to die from homicide, which has become the number one killer of African American males between the ages of fifteen and twenty-four. This crisis calls for immediate solution.

In Detroit, that solution took the form of an all-male academy, a concept I have advocated for the past few years and one which obviously reflects the collective spirit of the Detroit community. A similar concern was registered in a resolution passed by over 500 parents at a neighborhood school conference on at-risk students in March of 1990.

In the summer of 1990, the Detroit Board of Education accepted my proposal for the creation of a male academy and appointed a task force to refine the proposal during 1990-91. The underlying rationale

▲ Clifford Watson

of the male academy is that a unique school program is necessary to address the unique needs of urban males.

The Academy is based on the African-centered perspective that infuses African American culture, experience and contributions into all subject areas, including even foreign languages, science and computer and vocational technology, and extends to rites of passage and instruction in civic and community responsibility to complete the core curriculum. Given the research demonstrating the need for early intervention, the academy proposal targets students in the K through 5 population. Careful attention was given to the composition of the academy so as not to bias it toward any single class group. The admission policy provides for an even distribution of high-, medium-, and low-risk boys in the student population.

The proposal reflects the pioneer nature of this educational intervention model and calls for a prototype program and educational proving ground where educators can experiment with instructional strategies, curricula and programs to impact at-risk students throughout the entire educational system. This concept received such overwhelming and broad-based community support that the Detroit Board of Education created not one but three such academies to serve elementary school students. The first, MalcolmX Academy, opened in September 1991.

The Detroit School Board's response to the African American male's struggle for survival and educational equity caused controversy and a national debate about solutions to the African American male crisis, raised issues of educational equity for female students and triggered a Federal lawsuit. On August 22, 1991, just four days prior to the opening of the three Detroit academies, the American Civil Liberties Union (ACLU) and the National Organization for Women Legal Defense and Educational Fund (NOWLDEF) filed a lawsuit on behalf of three African American female students alleging that the establishment of all-male academies constituted discrimination based on sex. They requested a preliminary injunction to prevent the academies from opening. On August 15, 1991, Federal Judge George Woods granted the injunction and ordered the Detroit School Board to work out a compromise that would not discriminate

▲ Malcolm X Academy

against girls. The Detroit Board of Education took two courses of action:

- ☞ in a compromise with ACLU and NOWLDEF, it agreed to reopen admission to the academies and to admit approximately 136 girls to what are now termed "African-Centered Academies," and

- ☞ it opened three additional academies designed for girls but also open to males.

A WORD ABOUT AFRIKAN-CENTERED EDUCATION

Malik Yakini
Director of Nsoroma Institute
Highland Park, Michigan

The movement for Afrikan-centered education is dynamic and controversial. It is revitalizing our people's efforts of self-definition and empowerment. It is viewed by many black scholar-activists as a way to create a collective consciousness which can lead to empowerment and respect for our communities. It is characterized by its opponents as an attempt to further fragment the fragile ethnic and cultural fabric of American society.

The Afrikan-centered education movement has its roots in the struggles which took place throughout America in the 1960s and 1970s, for the inclusion of "black history" in the K-12 curriculum and for "black" and "Afro-American studies" programs in colleges and universities. These struggles in turn were influenced by black nationalist thinkers and activists of the 19th and early 20th centuries such as Martin Delany, Bishop Henry McNeal Turner and Marcus Garvey.

Afrikan-centered education has been advocated by numerous organizations, most notably the National Black United Front (NBUF), The Association for the Study of Classical Afrikan Civilizations (ASCAC), and The Council of Independent Black Institutions (CIBI). The more than twenty years of institution-building by CIBI has provided the model for the practice of Afrikan-centered education. Scholars such as Dr. Molefi Asante, Dr. John Henrik Clarke, Dr. Yosef ben-Jochanon, Dr. Marimba Aru, Dr. Asa Hilliard, III, and Dr. Jacob Carruthers have provided much of the historical and conceptual information upon which our movement rests. According to Kwame Agyei Akoto, Director of Nationhouse Watoto Shule and author of

▲ Afrikan-Centered High School students from Miami, Florida learn new and important facts about African American heritage.

the important book *Nationbuilding: The Theory and Practice in Afrikan-Centered Education*, Afrikan-centered education is practiced in two distinct ways—it takes the form of infusion in schools where there is an attempt to supplement the existing curriculum by including the contributions, achievements and perspectives of Afrikan peoples, and it is called *independent* in schools where the curriculum, environment and staff reflect a commitment to Afrikan cultural restoration.

Detroit is the leader in Afrikan-centered education nationally, with a strong tradition of independent Afrikan-centered schools. There are Sixteen Detroit Public Schools which have been designated as Afrikan-centered. Detroit Board of Education member Kwame Kenyatta is probably the only black nationalist on a public school board in a major U.S. city.

WHAT ARE THE OBJECTIVES OF PUBLIC EDUCATION IN AMERICA?

- to maintain European and Euro-American cultural dominance.

- to promote American patriotism in the form of blind obedience to authority, and the concept that "America must be number one" technologically, militarily, intellectually, politically and economically

- to produce workers and managers for the corporate and governmental sectors. The children of upper-middle-class communities are schooled to become managers, owners and operators of the corporate and governmental apparatus. The children of Black, Hispanic, Native American and other oppressed communities are trained to become workers, functionaries, and consumers within a system which someone else controls.

- to guarantee an "acceptable" level of unemployment, thereby creating competition for jobs and increased control of the work force

WHAT ARE THE OBJECTIVES OF AFRIKAN-CENTERED EDUCATION?

- to change the self-image of Afrikan people. This includes eliminating any sense of inferiority based on race, class or gender. Afrikan-centered education seeks to develop a view of ourselves as whole, capable human beings.

- to restore a way of thinking, speaking and acting which upholds the sacredness of nature and the harmony, balance and order of its parts. The ancient Kemetic people (Egyptians) called this understanding *Ma'at*.

🜋 to develop a cadre of thinkers, workers, scholars and organizers capable of changing the social, economic and political status of Afrikan people

WHAT ARE THE CHARACTERISTICS OF AFRIKAN-CENTERED EDUCATION?

🜋 to view Afrikans as the prototypes of humanity, the original model from which the various branches of humankind developed

🜋 to put human history in its proper perspective by upholding the Afrikan origin of civilization. Afrikan-centered education puts particular emphasis on the importance of Kemet and other classical Afrikan civilizations

🜋 whenever possible, to use sources and references which are Afrikan

🜋 to occur in an environment which reflects our history and culture

🜋 to be provided by teachers who reflect a commitment to excellence and Afrikan cultural restoration

🜋 to promote a holistic approach to learning and to combine varied disciplines into a harmonious whole

🜋 to seek to develop the whole person, mentally, physically, spiritually

🜋 to take into account the right brain dominant learning style and the varied types of intelligence of Afrikans

🜋 to use a multimodal approach to teaching knowledge and skills

🜋 to utilize cooperative learning and encourage the sharing of knowledge and resources

🜋 to be responsive to the needs and aspirations of Afrikan people and to prepare us for empowerment and self-determination

THE SPIRITUALITY OF AFRIKAN-CENTERED EDUCATION

Each child is a unique manifestation of divine spirit with particular gifts, personality traits and needs. This understanding must guide our interactions with our children and must illuminate our attempts to develop appropriate curriculum and instruction for them. As Afrikan-

Malik Yakini

centered parents and educators, our job must be to recognize "who" each child is. Our responsibility is to expose our children to the proper combination of spiritual, mental and physical experiences.

We have been taught to buy into the mind-set which European American capitalism has created through compulsory public school education. Students are expected to know a specific set of facts and academic skills according to very rigid, age-based standards, for example, that every first grade student should be reading. Perhaps some first graders are not yet ready to pursue such a serious endeavor. Perhaps some children would be better served by being allowed to spend the first grade forming and shaping clay or planting and caring for a garden. Every child is unique. Our job must be to allow each soul to unfold.

Many parents, in their zeal for academic progress, push their children to perform on levels which do not take into account the total development of the child. In our attempts to adhere to the societal "norm," we impose unnatural conditions on our children such as expecting them to sit still in desks for long periods of time. Perhaps the destiny of a particular child involves a great deal of physical movement. That child should not be negatively labeled if he or she does not easily fit into the box which we have prepared for them.

Traditional Afrikan education utilized means of divining or reading the spiritual destiny of each child and the challenges that child was likely to face in life, thus a prescription for what would be beneficial and what would be harmful was developed for each child. The child would be exposed to particular experiences at the prescribed time. The context and relations into which the child was born and lived was made clear.

While it is very difficult within the context of this society to completely implement such traditional practices, Afrikan-centered educators must develop a sensitivity for the needs and gifts of each child we teach. Our objectives must be to facilitate the development of each child's potential and to promote Afrikan self-reliance through the acquisition of the skills and knowledge which we deem important for nation building and maintenance.